THEY DIDN'T REALLY MEAN IT!

A BOOK OF BOOBS AND BLUNDERS

CORGI BOOKS

THEY DIDN'T REALLY MEAN IT
A CORGI BOOK   0 552 13319 1

First publication in Great Britain

PRINTING HISTORY
Corgi Edition published 1987

Copyright © 1987 Russell Ash & Bernard Higton

Illustrations by Ellis Nadler

Corgi Books are published by Transworld Publishers Ltd.,
61-63 Uxbridge Road, Ealing, London W5 5SA,
in Australia by Transworld Publishers (Australia) Pty. Ltd.,
15-23 Helles Avenue, Moorebank, NSW 2170,
and in New Zealand by Transworld Publishers (NZ) Ltd.,
Cnr Moselle and Waipareira Avenues, Henderson, Auckland.

Printed and bound in Great Britain by
Hazell Watson & Viney Limited,
Member of the BPCC Group,
Aylesbury, Bucks

CONTENTS

BOOK BOOBS

Titillating Titles
Lit-Slips
The Bard's Boobs
Poetry In Motion

TITILLATING TITLES
Unusual (and authentic) books for the discerning reader

Small Organs in Holland
G. Verloop, 1978

COME PLAY IN MY TUNNEL
Dorothy Aaronson

SUCCESS WITH SMALL FRUITS
Edward Payson Roe, 1880

ABOUT RAW JUICES
John Benedict Lust, 1962

NANCY GOES CAMPING
Jean Henry Large, 1931

DICK'S FAIRY
Silas Kito Hocking, 1883

The Nature and Tendency of Balls
Jacob Ide, 1818

Handbook for the Limbless
Geoffrey Howson, 1922

A French Letter Writing Guide
D. Sephton, 1980

Mated with a Clown
Lady Constance Howard, 1884

Queer Pets and their Doings
Oliver Miller, 1880

Physical Properties of Slags
Commission of the European Communities on
Technical Steel Research, 1981

Some Account of my Intercourse
with Madame Blavatsky from 1872 to 1884
Madame E. Coulomb, 1885

Come Rest Your Head on these Two
Evelyn Hamlin

The Romance of Three Bachelors
Helen Harding, 1895

The Story of Johnnies
(A History of the Johannesburg Consolidated Investment Co.)

Play with Your Own Marbles
J. J. Wright, 1880

Fairies at Work and Play
Geoffrey Hodson, 1925

Prematurely Gay
Jack Iams, 1951

The Complete Troller
Robert Nobbes, 1682

Be Married and Like It
Bernarr Macfadden, 1937

Whippings and Lashings
The Girl Guide's Association, 1977

Fanny's First, or Tender Trifles
W. Brown Kitchener, 1829

Forrester's Fag
Alfred Judd, 1926

Inflammatory Bowel Diseases: A Personal View
Henry D. Janowitz, 1985

Grandfather Was Queer
Richardson Wright, 1939

Flashes from the Welsh Pulpit
Rev. J. Gwynoro Davies, 1889

A Girl's Ride in Iceland
Ethel Brilliana Tweedie, 1889

A Love Passage
Lady Harriet Phillimore, 1908

The Line of Cleavage Under Elizabeth
Dom Norbert Birt, 1909

An Irish Tourist Board Publication

The Toothbrush: Its Use and Abuse
Isador Hirschfield, 1939

Five Queer Women
Walter Copeland Jerrold and Clare Jerrold, 1929

Warfare in the Enemy's Rear
Otto Heilbrunn, 1963

Mated with a Clown
Lady Constance Howard, 1884

The Last Agony of the Great Bore
F. W. Bird, 1868

British Tits
Christopher Perrins, 1979

Shag the Caribou
C. Bernard Rutley, 1949 (In series with *Peeko the Beaver*)

Our Vice: Regal Life in India
(Lady Dufferin's *Our Vice-Regal Life in India*,
as printed in a bookseller's catalogue)

The Joystick
('The Organ of A. V. Roe & Co.', 1917-20)

Sporting Bits
(A magazine published in the 1890s)

Report of the Committee on Relations with Junior Members
(*Oxford University Gazette*, 1969)

Kinki Women Make World's Best Wives
(An article in a 1962 tourist guide to the
Kinki region of Japan)

LIT-SLIPS
Classic blunders of authors

On entering the drawing-room, she found the whole party at loo, and was immediately invited to join them.
(Jane Austen, *Pride and Prejudice*, 1813)

———o———

Certainly, my home at my uncle's brought me acquainted with a circle of admirals. Of *Rears* and *Vices*, I saw enough.
(Jane Austen, *Mansfield Park*, 1814)

Mrs Goddard was the mistress of a School – not of a seminary, or an establishment, or any thing which professed, in long sentences of refined nonsense, to combine liberal acquirements with elegant morality upon new principles and new systems – and where young ladies for enormous pay might be screwed out of health and into vanity. . .
(Jane Austen, *Emma*, 1816)

———o———

Thou shalt commit adultery.
(Exodus xx.14 – printed thus in the so-called 'Wicked Bible' of 1631)

———o———

Self Abuse: The great thing to do, after having solemnly vowed never to give up the struggle, is to take hold of one's self.
(Rose Woodallen Chapman, *In Her Teens*, 1914)

———o———

Like Adela, he had dark brown hair, with enormous black eyebrows, a moustache, and a short beard.
(Thomas Cobb, *A Marriage of Inconvenience*, 1913)

———o———

He had been aware from the first that she was unusually attractive; now, in her dark green dress with the low-cut, rounded neckline, he saw that she had lovely legs.
(George Harmon Coxe, *The Jade Venus*, 1947)

———o———

No public business of any kind could possibly be done at any time, without the acquiescence of the Circumlocution Office. Its finger was in the largest public pie, and in the smallest public tart.
(Charles Dickens, *Little Dorrit*, 1855-7)

———○———

17 November 1753. Soon after came the Prince of Wales, and Prince Edward; and then the Lady Augusta, all in an undress and took their stools and sat round the fire with us.
(George Bubb Dodington's *Diary*, 1784)

———○———

Charmian: Help, chafe her temples, Iras.
Iras: Bend, bend her forward quickly.
Charmian: Heaven be praised! She comes again.
(John Dryden, *All for Love*, 1678)

———○———

Mrs Glegg had doubtless the glossiest and crispest brown curls in her drawers, as well as curls in various degrees of fuzzy laxness.
(George Eliot, *The Mill on the Floss*, 1860)

———○———

When she spoke, Tom held his breath, so eagerly he listened; when she sang, he sat like one entranced. She touched his organ and from that bright epoch, even it, the old companion of his happiest hours, incapable as he had thought of elevation, began a new and deified existence. . . I deeply appreciate his talent for the organ, notwithstanding that I do not, if I may use the expression, grind myself.
(Charles Dickens, *Martin Chuzzlewit*, 1843-4)

———○———

'Shall *I* take the organ out?'
Old Treffy did not answer: a great struggle was going on in his mind. Could he let anyone but himself touch his dear old organ?
(Catherine Augusta Walton, *Christie's Old Organ*, 1882)

Angels have no right to come, even as
errands of mercy, in a nude condition.
(Rev. J. J. Fleharty, quoted in Major Seton Churchill,
Forbidden Fruit for Young Men, 1887)

———————o———————

Harley also employed Defoe to write *The
Review*, and St John had his own organ in
the *Post Boy*.
(R. W. Harris, *England in the Eighteenth Century*,
1963)

———————o———————

'Well!' said the Duchess to me, 'apart from
your balls, can't I be of any use to you?'
(Marcel Proust, *Cities of the Plain*, 1921-22)

———————o———————

. . . I never made advances to a woman
who wouldn't have gladly acknowledged to
thirty-five. And I give them love. Why,
many of them had never known what it was
to have a man do them up behind.
(Somerset Maugham, *The Round Dozen*, 1939)

———————o———————

'Oh, I can't explain!' cried Roderick
impatiently, returning to his work. 'I've
only one way of expressing my deepest
feelings – it's this.' And he swung his tool.
(Henry James, *Roderick Hudson*, 1876)

———————o———————

You think me a queer fellow already. It's
not easy, either, to tell you what I feel –
not easy for so queer a fellow as I to tell
you in how many ways he's queer.
(Henry James, *A Passionate Pilgrim*, 1875)

Our parents had gone there for a year or
two to be near our grandmother on their
return from their first visit to Europe,
which had quite immediately followed my
birth, which appears to have lasted some
year and a half, and of which I shall have
another word to say.
(Henry James, *A Small Boy and Others*, 1913)

———————o———————

Mr Longdon, resisting, kept erect with a
low gasp that his host only was near
enough to catch. This suddenly appeared
to confirm an impression gathered by
Vanderbank in their contact, a strange
sense that his visitor was so agitated as to
be trembling in every limb. It brought to
his lips a kind of ejaculation.
(Henry James, *The Awkward Age*, 1899)

———————o———————

Meredith had an unbounded enthusiasm for
French letters as such. 'He lost his sense
of proportion in that matter,' said Henry
James to Alice Meynell.
(Note in *George Meredith's Letters to Alice Meynell*,
1923)

———————o———————

Wednesday 21 January 1801. I dined at
Deane yesterday, as I told you I should; –
& met the two Mr Holders. – We played at
Vingt-un, which as Fulwar was
unsuccessful, gave him an opportunity of
exposing himself as usual.
(Jane Austen, letter to her sister, Cassandra)

It was observed that, at this particular crossing,
in nearly every case, the time allowed for
crossing was adequate, but there was great anxiety
when the Green Man started flashing.
(Report by Hounslow Borough Engineer)

A man who exposes himself when he is intoxicated has not the art of getting drunk.
(Samuel Johnson, quoted in James Boswell's *The Life of Samuel Johnson*, 1791)

————○————

The confidence which presumes to do, by surveying the surface, what labour can perform, by penetrating the bottom.
(Samuel Johnson, preface to his edition of Shakespeare's *Works*, 1765)

And when you had found him, you found a man superficially coy, perhaps, but at bottom always ready to do business.
(Charles Reade, *It is Never Too Late to Mend*, 1856)

————○————

Having for years had no real intercourse with any one save his wife, he was very shy.
(Dame Ethel Smyth, *Impressions that Remained*, 1919)

————○————

The stillness of the hour is the stillness of a dead clam at sea.
(Austin Phelps, *The Still Hour*, 1860 – it should have read 'calm')

————○————

7 June 1871. I'm not going to offer – still less urge – marriage, now. But I insist on free intercourse – face to face.
(John Ruskin, letter to William Cowper-Temple)

————○————

19 November 1846. No woman was happier in her choice – no woman – And after above two months of uninterrupted intercourse, there is still more and more cause for thankfulness; – and more and more affection on his side – He loves me better every day, he says. . . My health improves still, too.
(Elizabeth Barrett Browning, letter to Hugh Stuart Boyd)

———⚬———

She gave a little scream and a jerk, and so relieved herself.
(Anthony Trollope, *The Duke's Children*, 1880)

———⚬———

From my window I saw them running through the garden in every direction, embracing each other, ejaculating, playing, and counting their beads, with hands tremulous and eyes uplifted in ecstasy.
(Charles Robert Maturin, *Melmoth the Wanderer*, 1820)

———⚬———

Miss Sedley's new *femme de chambre* refused to go to bed without a wax candle.
(William Makepeace Thackeray, *Vanity Fair*, 1847-8)

———⚬———

Mr Grant, really glad of an excuse to dismount, offered his cock to Lydia, who immediately flung a leg over it, explaining that she had put on a frock with pleats on purpose.
(Angela Thirkell, *The Brandons*, 1939)

A deep armchair stood before the fireplace. She took it up between thumb and forefinger, handling it delicately, set it down on the other side, and considered it profoundly.
(Fanny Heaslip Lea, *Wild Goose Chase*, 1929)

17

Well now, you look here, that was a good lay of your last night. I don't deny it was a good lay. Some of you are pretty handy with a hand-spike end.
(Robert Louis Stevenson, *Treasure Island*, 1883)

The Food (Sector Scheme) Order, 1943, as amended, shall be further amended by inserting in the Second Schedule thereto, the entry, 'Nuts'.
(Ministry of Food directive, 1945)

THE BARD'S BOOBS
What Shakespeare didn't mean to say

I must go up and down like a cock that nobody can match.
(*Cymbeline*)

Trib, trib, fairies: come; and remember your parts.
(*Merry Wives of Windsor*)

If you can penetrate her with your fingering, so; we'll try with tongue too.
(*Cymbeline*)

I partly know the instrument that screws me.
(*Twelfth Night*)

Gregory: Draw thy tool; here comes two of the house of the Montagues.
Sampson: My naked weapon is out.
(*Romeo and Juliet*)

My lord, she may be a punk.
(*Measure for Measure*)

I do see the bottom of Justice Shallow.
(*Henry IV* Pt. 2)

We are come off like Romans.
(*Coriolanus*)

So did I abuse myself.
(*Twelfth Night*)

Pistol's cock is up.
(*Henry V*)

POETRY IN MOTION
Raunchy rhymes for dirty minds

So 'tis with Christians, Nature being weak,
While in this world, are liable to leak.
(William Balmford, *The Seaman's Spiritual Companion*, 1678)

On barren mountains doth Adonis lie,
A boar's white tusk hat gored his whiter
   thigh:
His short pants Venus grieve.
(Bion, *Lament for Adonis*, trans. Thomas Stanley, 1651)

She touched the organ; – I could stand
   For hours and hours. . .
(Winthrop Mackworth Praed, *The Belle of the Ball-room*, 1831)

The organ 'gins to swell;
   She's coming, she's coming!
My lady comes at last. . .
   I will not enter there.
(William Makepeace Thackeray, *At the Church Gate*, 1849-50)

Soon shalt thou hear the Bridegroom's
    voice,
The midnight cry, 'Behold, I come!'
(Horatius Bonar, 'Go labour on', Hymn 304 in the
Public School Hymn Book, 1920)

———o———

You brush it, till I grow aware,
    Who wants me, and wide ope I burst.
(Robert Browning, *In a Gondola*, 1845)

———o———

    Sebald, as we lay,
Rising and falling only with our pants. . .
(Robert Browning, *Pippa Passes*, 1841)

———o———

Then, owls and bats
Cowls and twats,
Monks and nuns, in a cloister's moods
Adjourn to the oak-stump pantry.
(Robert Browning, *Pippa Passes*, 1841 – Browning
explained to the editor of the *Oxford English
Dictionary* that he thought a 'twat' was a kind of hood
worn by nuns.)

———o———

One moment may with bliss repay
    Unnumbered hours of pain;
Such was the sob and the mutual throb
    Of the knight embracing Jane.
(Thomas Campbell, *The Ritter Bann*, 1824)

———o———

A fly, that up and down himself doth shove.
(William Wordsworth, *To Sleep*, 1806)

———o———

And when you'd a mind to career
Off anywhere – say to town –
You were all on a sudden gone
Before I had thought thereon,
Or noticed your trunks were down.
(Thomas Hardy, *Without Ceremony*, 1912-13)

———o———

True a woman was found the day ensuing,
    And some at times averred
The grave to be her false one's, who when
    wooing
    Gave her the bird.
(Thomas Hardy, *Within a Churchyard*)

———o———

    Forlornly, silently,
Plays in the evening garden
    Myself with me.
(Walter de la Mare, *Myself*, 1906)

———o———

Fairy muffs are made of pussy-willow.
(*The Rose Fyleman Fairy Book*, 1923)

———o———

Cock up your beaver, and cock it fu'
    sprush!
We'll over the Border and gie them a
    brush:
There's somebody there we'll teach better
    behaviour,
Hey, brave Johnnie lad, cock up your
    beaver!
(Robert Burns, *Cock up your Beaver*)

———o———

O Moon! when I look on thy beautiful face,
Careering along through the boundaries of space,
The thought has frequently come into my mind,
If ever I'll gaze on thy glorious behind.
(Anon.; attributed to Edmund Gosse's housemaid)

Then her cheek was pale and thinner than
    should be for one so young,
And her eye on all my motions with a mute
    observance hung.
(Alfred Tennyson, *Locksley Hall*, 1842)

———○———

Whate'er is done in this sweet isle,
    There's none that may not lift his horn,
If only lifted with a smile.
(William Johnson Cory, author of the 'Eton Boating
Song', 'A Queen's Visit' in *Ionica*, 1858)

———○———

Go, spend your penny, Beauty, when you
    will,
In the grave's darkness let the stamp be
    lost.
The water still will bubble. . .
(John Masefield, *Lollingdon Downs and other Poems –
Sonnet LXVII*, 1917)

———○———

Her beauty smoothed earth's furrow'd
    face!
    She gave me tokens three: –
A look, a word of her winsome mouth,
    And a wild raspberry.
(Francis Thompson, *Daisy*, 1893)

———○———

How brave a prospect is a bright backside!
(Henry Vaughan, *Silex Scintillatus: Sacred Poems and
Private Ejaculations*, 1655)

———○———

For me are homelier tasks prepared.
To the stone table in my garden
The Squire is come, and as I guess,
His pretty little daughter Bess
With Harry the Churchwarden.
(William Wordsworth, original version of his prologue
to *Peter Bell*, 1819)

———○———

Gay go up and gay go down.
(Anon., *The Bells of London*)

———○———

Hold it up, show it, bring the torch!
(Euripides, *Cassandra's Epithalmium*)

———○———

On a lavatory, below, sat a cherub.
(Longfellow, *Hyperion*, 1838)

———○———

"...AND NOW FOR SOMETHING COMPLETELY DIFFERENT"

Radio, TV and other live lapses

Apparently the Florida vacation did him a lot of good. Ike (President Eisenhower) returned today looking fanned and tit.
(US broadcaster Walter Cronkite)

———◇———

There is good news on the war front tonight. From North Africa comes word that Allied troops have stopped the advances of Hitler's Pansy Division.
(BBC radio announcement, 1942)

———◇———

The batsman's Holding, the bowler's Willey.
(Brian Johnston, commentary on 1976 Test, England v. West Indies at the Oval, re: Michael Holding and Peter Willey)

———◇———

Our girls like booze in any form – pardon me, that should be blues.
(Ina Ray Hutton introducing her all-girl orchestra on NBC-TV)

———◇———

Former Wimbledon champion Martina Navratilova had a surprisingly easy victory over Andrea Jaeger in the final of the Avon Tournament in Seattle. She won in straight sex.
(BBC radio newsreader)

———◇———

Stick your finger in the operator's hole and – er, the telephone hole marked 'Operator', that is, and call in now.
(Disc jockey on Radio KCBQ, San Diego, California)

Johan Kriek, the number ten seed in the American Open Tennis Tournament being played at Flushing Meadows, New York, has been bitten – has been beaten, I should say, by Ilie Nastasie of Romania.
(BBC radio newsreader)

———◇———

President Ronald Reagan is alive and well and kicking tonight, one day after the assassination attempt, just two-and-a-half months into his pregnancy.
(US newsreader)

———◇———

I am pretty sure Queen Mary's arriving because I can see her motorcycle.
(John Snagge, spotting Her Majesty's motorcycle escort, in a pre-War BBC radio commentary on the Aldershot Tattoo)

———◇———

The FA Cup Final has forced colourful politician, Pat Wall, to shave off his beard. The Militant supporter is an Everton fanatic, and said that unless they won the Cup, he'd keep his distinctive bristols for ever – *bristles* for ever!
(BBC radio newsreader)

———◇———

So let's look at Major Petch's erection – or perhaps I should call it Major Petch's stand.
(Lord John Oaksey, inviting TV viewers to examine an embankment built by Clerk of the Course, Major Petch, at York Racecourse)

———◇———

First of all *Horizon* on BBC2 tonight is
doing a programme about the motorcycle,
Survival of the Fartest.
(Richard Baker)

And back from the news we come to *Fever* from Leggy Pee.
(Don Wardell announcing Peggy Lee on *Music in the Night*, Radio Luxembourg)

————◇————

And there she is, the whole vast bulk of her.
(As the aircraft carrier, *Ark Royal*, was launched, Wynford Vaughan-Thomas was describing the ship to BBC television viewers – just as the camera switched to the Queen Mother)

————◇————

From the fifties, a re-release for Bill Haley and the Comets, *Rock around the Cock*.
(Disc jockey on WCCB, Clarion, Pennsylvania)

————◇————

(Rehearsal for an episode of BBC TV's *Dixon of Dock Green*)

TAKE ONE:

Nolan: Where is it? Now don't just stand there – give!
Weasel: I haven't got it, Mr Nolan.
Nolan: Now listen, Weasel: if I don't get that necklace back *right* now, they'll never be able to put you together again!
Weasel: I haven't got it! It's down at Dock Green Dick!
Nolan: The *nick*!

TAKE TWO:

Weasel: I haven't got it! It's down at Dick Green Dock!
(*aside*) Can't I just say, 'the nick'?

Protest demonstrations have taken place by workers whose trade union rights have been betrayed, by Catholics whose freedom of expression has been circumcised – circumscribed.
(Adlai Stevenson, US radio broadcast)

————◇————

Wynford Vaughan Thomas: How do you think she [Eleanor Roosevelt, during wartime visit to Britain] will be received?
Interviewee: With all the heartfelt fervour of a brother nation struggling for its survival.
WVT: Are you hoping to see her yourself?
Interviewee: Alas, no. I understand that only the United States Forces in this country are going to have intercourse with her.

————◇————

. . . the band playing, people picnicking round the ground, while on the field hundreds of small boys are playing with their balls.
(Rex Alston, cricket commentary)

————◇————

How is the World Cock sucker team doing?
(Ron Hunter on Channel 10, Miami, Florida, attempting to enquire about the World Cup soccer team)

————◇————

At 8.50 tonight, we shall be broadcasting Haydn's *Cremation*.
(Announcer on BBC Radio 3)

Don't go away folks. After the break we'll have a wildlife expert here, and he's going to show us a horny owl.
(Johnny Carson, *The Johnny Carson Show*)

———◇———

And Dad will love Wonder Bread's delicious flavour too. Remember, it's Wonder Bread for the breast in bed.
(US radio commercial)

———◇———

The next programme comes to you from the bathroom at Pump – I mean the Pumproom at Bath.
(Announcer on BBC Third Programme)

———◇———

In the next programme we'll be looking at blind dogs for the guide.
(Simon Grooms on *Blue Peter*, BBC TV)

From his emergency flood headquarters at City Hall, Mayor Friedman has just ordered all families living near or adjacent to the Mill River to ejaculate immediately.
(Dave Duncan, Radio WLKW, Rhode Island)

———◇———

On the local news scene the shitty sherrif,
I mean the City Sherrif, was kept busy
with three buglers last night – *burglars*!
(Radio KUTY, Palmdale, California)

Why is it that I'm always enthusiastic about the music of Johann Strauss, and always sleep with Aida?
(Musicologist Dr Sigmund Spaeth on US radio programme)

———◇———

And now parading before us is a lovely beverage of booties.
(Skitch Henderson, *Miss US* commentary on NBC-TV)

———◇———

Here to speak on behalf of the Labour party is Sir Stifford Crapps.
(Macdonald Hobley on BBC TV, 1949)

———◇———

Well, the streakers are at it again, this time at a local football game just outside of Boston. I can't figure out this type of behaviour – I guess it's their way of showing they're nuts.
(Larry Glick, WBZ News, Boston, Massachusetts)

———◇———

Ladies and gentlemen, Mr Eddie Playbody will now pee for you.
(US announcer introducing banjoist Eddie Peabody)

———◇———

In response to complaints from the touring company of *Oh, Calcutta!*, the nude review, that they were suffering from the cold, the theatre management have agreed to install fan heaters.
(BBC Radio 4 News, 1981)

And now Nelson Eddy sings *While My Lady Sleeps* with the men's chorus.
(Announcer on KALW, San Francisco, California)

———◇———

Well, that was the forecast, and we're sorry for the F in Fog.
(Julian Pettifer, following a TV weather forecast in which the chart omitted the letter 'F' from 'Fog')

———◇———

Hunt's Furniture Store has Davey Crockett beds – it's a twin-size bed, just right for the kids – with scenes of Davey Crockett in action on the mattress.
(US radio commercial)

———◇———

. . . His Popiness the Hole.
(US newscaster on the Pope's visit to the USA)

———◇———

Do you think the prisoners will regard you as a good screw?
(Jack de Manio interviewing a female assistant prison governor)

———◇———

Henry Horeton's got a funny sort of stance. It looks as if he is shitting on a sooting stick.
(Brian Johnston, cricket commentary)

———◇———

The next song will be *I've Seen Everything when I've Seen an Elephant's Fly.*
(US radio disc jockey)

———◇———

Connors' wife is expecting a baby and there was some doubt about his entry.
(Peter West describing the Wimbledon entrants)

———⋄———

Steinberg's Department Store has just received a shipment of large bathing suits. Ladies, now you can buy a bathing suit for a ridiculous figure!
(US radio commercial)

———⋄———

When you're through with your old bag, just discard her, er, I mean *it*.
(Arthur Godfrey, Lipton's Tea commercial on CBS)

This is KTIW, Sexas Titty – Texas City!

———⋄———

And now the Queen's gone round the bend.
(Henry Riddell, commentating on a royal procession)

———⋄———

. . . I am, of course, a great Willey supporter.
(Trevor Bailey on cricketer Peter Willey)

———⋄———

. . . the Government's gay pidelines.
(Angela Rippon – on pay guidelines – BBC TV News)

———⋄———

Be sure to see *Pretty Maids All in a Row*, headed by Rock Hudson and directed by Roger Vadim, the man who uncovered Brigitte Bardot and Jane Fonda.
(Wilson Hatcher, Channel 41, Louisville, Kentucky)

———⋄———

People behind Martina Navratilova on the roller have the best view of her receiving service.
(Max Robertson, BBC radio commentary)

———⋄———

As Big Ben's cock strikes eleven, it's time for the news.
(BBC announcer)

———⋄———

There's Neil Harvey, standing at slip with his legs wide apart, waiting for a tickle.
(Brian Johnston, commentating on Test Match, Headingley, 1961)

At Oxford Crown Court today, Donald Nielsen denied being the Pink Panther.
(Edward Cole, BBC Radio 4 News)

Millions of people who have never died before will be killed!
(Captain Kirk, *Star Trek*)

Near to me is one of these special King's police in his Tudor finery. These men are called Beefburgers, and each one holds a halibut in his hand.
(US radio commentary on the wedding of Princess Elizabeth and Prince Philip, 20 November 1947)

Richard Whiteley: What's it like to be married?
Young bride: I can't say – it hasn't sunk in properly yet.
(*Calendar*, Yorkshire Television, 1972)

When that royal pair left the garden at midnight, after a great success, that handsome Prince Charming from England left there, on the lawns, a whole string of enchanted ravished ladies.
(Unnamed Guyanan commentator on the visit of Queen and Prince Philip)

As you come over to join us, Ray Illingworth has just relieved himself at the Pavilion end.
(Brian Johnston, cricket commentary)

———◇———

You've just missed seeing Barry Richards hit one of Basil D'Oliveira's balls clean out of the ground.
(Brian Johnston, cricket commentary)

———◇———

At 1:45 London Weekend brings you *University Challenge*, followed at 2:15 by an in-depth leak into the FA Cup – *look* into the FA Cup final!
(ITV announcer)

———◇———

Yorkshire 232 all out; Hutton ill. I am sorry – Hutton 111.
(John Savage, BBC radio news)

———◇———

And now for a favourite song of mine and I'm sure of yours – *Everybloody Loves Somebloody Sometime*.
(Danny Street, *Easybeat*, BBC radio)

———◇———

According to Enoch Powell, MP for Wolverhampton, the pound will suffer further fuckuation before it stabilizes.
(Radio news)

———◇———

Stick your courage to the screwing place.
(Lady Macbeth, in a radio production of *Macbeth*)

It's a very close race. I can't see who's in the lead, it's either Oxford or Cambridge.
(John Snagge commenting on the 1949 Oxford & Cambridge Boat Race)

———◇———

And now, Whoopee John Wilfahrt and the Orchestra will play.
(US radio announcer)

———◇———

It's extremely cold here. The England fielders are keeping their hands in their pockets between balls.
(Christopher Martin-Jenkins, commentary on the 1979 Cricket World Cup, England v. Canada)

———◇———

Finally, 38 million Spaniards have been experiencing their first erection for 40 years.
(Don Durbridge, Radio 2 News, on Spain's first post-Franco election)

———◇———

Well, that's close of play here, with Hampshire 301 all out. But they go on playing till seven o'clock at Edgbaston, so over there now for some more balls from Rex Alston.
(Brian Johnston, radio cricket commentary)

———◇———

In a concentrated effort to apprehend the rapist, local police have asked all women in the area to copulate with them – *cooperate* with them.
(Unnamed US announcer)

32

This portion of the news is brought to you by Quick Strip grocery
store, where we can service your every need.
(Quick Trip grocery store commercial on Radio KTUL, Tulsa, Oklahoma)

I have just learned that we do have the film
of the astronauts' breakfast, which should
be coming up shortly.
(Frank McGee, NBC News, on a Gemini space mission)

Richard Kershaw: Sir Alan, do you feel circumcised by your restricted powers?
Ombudsman, Sir Alan Marre: You could put it that way. My powers are somewhat limited.
(*Newsnight*, BBC2, 1976)

———————◇———————

Here comes Juantorena now. Every time the big Cuban opens his legs, he shows his class.
(Ron Pickering, BBC TV commentary on the Montreal Olympics)

———————◇———————

And Helena got six inches during the night – Helena, Montana, that is!
(Snow report on Radio KHAR, Alaska)

———————◇———————

This is David Hamilton bidding you good night, and a reminder for you to be sure to turn off your sex.
(David Hamilton, closing down BBC TV for the night)

———————◇———————

Let's hope all your doughnuts come out as Fanny's.
(Frank Bough, re: TV cook Fanny Craddock)

———————◇———————

I've covered topless bathing suits, bottomless bathing suits, and now I've got Pussy Galore.
(US TV interviewer introducing Honor Blackman, co-star in the 1964 James Bond film, *Goldfinger*)

———————◇———————

It's eleven o'clock on the English Service, and here is the nude – I beg your pardon, here is the news, read by Stella Heyer.

———————◇———————

We're going to play a hiding and finding game with the music. Now this is what we do: we pretend that you've got some balls, and I'm going to hide them. They might be hidden high up near the ceiling (*madly tinkling piano*) – or, they might be hidden low down, on the floor (*thunderously deep piano*). You don't know where I'm going to hide your balls – but the music will tell you. Now, first of all, shut your eyes while I hide them. Yes – shut your eyes. Now, open your eyes – and dance lightly about, looking everywhere for your balls (*dance music plays*). And now the music's going to tell you where your balls are. They may be high up, so that you have to stretch and jump up for them, or they may be low down, so that you have to pick them up off the floor. Listen – (*madly tinkling piano*). Well, were your balls high up or low down? They were high up! And I hope you've all jumped up and got them. Now, dance round and toss them up in the air, and play with them (*jolly ball-tossing music plays*). Now I'm going to hide the balls again. Shut your eyes. Now open them. And run lightly round, looking everywhere for your balls (*dance music plays again*).
(Isobel Anne Shead, *Listen with Mother*, BBC radio, 1930s)

35

A lady switched on her radio and distinctly heard someone say, 'Great tits like coconuts'. Outraged, she switched off immediately and wrote a strong letter of complaint to Lord Reith, then Director-General of the BBC, who replied, 'Dear Madam, If you had only continued listening, you would have heard that robins like worms.'

―――――◇―――――

(Princess Margaret) . . . radiant in an off-the-hat face.
(Max Robertson, BBC radio commentary)

―――――◇―――――

Billie Jean King has always been conscious of wind on the centre court.
(Dan Maskell, Wimbledon commentary on BBC TV)

―――――◇―――――

Good-night. And don't forget to put your cocks back.
(Jimmy Hill, BBC TV)

―――――◇―――――

Visit our Coin-o-Matic Laundry. All ladies who drop off their clothing will receive prompt attention.
(US radio advertisement)

―――――◇―――――

Lady Margaret and Jesus are rowing neck and neck – no, Jesus is now making water in Lady Margaret!
(BBC radio commentator during Henley Royal Regatta)

Tonight, see Eugene O'Neill's *Long Day's Journey Into Night,* brought to you in its original, uncut virgin.
(Announcer on WRR-FM, Dallas)

―――――◇―――――

I took one arm, my colleague took the other arm – then we disarmed her.
(Policeman on BBC television's *Panorama*)

―――――◇―――――

Questionmaster: What is a sporran?
Game show contestant: I know what it is, but I can't define it.
Questionmaster: You only have 30 seconds left.
Contestant: It's that thing all covered with hair that hangs down between a Scotsman's legs!
(Canadian game show)

―――――◇―――――

Over now to Nigel Starmer-Smith who has had seven craps as scum-half for England.
(Jimmy Hill)

―――――◇―――――

President Carter has painful haemorrhoids and is being treated by his physician, Rear Admiral William Lookass – Lukash!
(US newscaster)

―――――◇―――――

The Lord Mayor's Show, which celebrates the erection of the new Lord Mayor of London, takes place annually . . .
(Unnamed TV commentator)

. . . a new film by Jacques Cousteau,
the famous French underwear explorer.
(Channel 13, New York)

Will it jerk me off?
(Margaret Thatcher, inspecting a field gun)

———————◇———————

Interviewer: What do you desire most, now that your husband has retired, Mme de Gaulle?
Mme de Gaulle: A penis.
Interviewer: A penis!?
Mme de Gaulle: Yes, great ha-penis. . .

———————◇———————

To you, and the people you represent, the great people of the government of Israel.
(Gerald Ford, at a Washington DC reception in 1975 – toasting President Anwar Sadat – of Egypt)

———————◇———————

. . . a great man who should have been President and would have been one of the greatest Presidents in history – Hubert Horatio Hornblower."
(Jimmy Carter at the 1980 Democratic Convention, attempting to speak about Hubert Humphrey)

———————◇———————

This is a great day for France.
(Richard Nixon at the 1974 funeral of President Georges Pompidou)

———————◇———————

That is a discredited president.
(Richard Nixon, trying to say 'discredited precedent', during the Watergate enquiry, 1974)

———————◇———————

Ladies and gentlemen, the President of the United States, Hoobert Heever!
(Harry Von Zell)

The United States has much to offer the third world war.
(Ronald Reagan speaking about the Third World, 1975)

———————◇———————

John Patten, in a speech in the House of Commons, tried to make a reference to the private rented sector. It came out as 'private scented rector'.

———————◇———————

The policeman isn't there to create disorder. The policeman is there to preserve disorder.
(Mayor Richard J. Daley of Chicago, 1968)

———————◇———————

The police are fully able to meet and compete with the criminals.
(Mayor John F. Hylan of NYC, 1922)

———————◇———————

My heart is as black as yours.
(Mario Procaccino running for mayor of New York, 1969, addressing a group of black people. He did not win.)

———————◇———————

Now let's all try to settle this problem in a true Christian spirit.
(Senator Warren Austin at the United Nations, on the Arab-Israeli conflict, 1948)

———————◇———————

My name is Raquel Welch. . . I am here for Visual Effects. . . And I have two of them. . . I mean nominations.
(1969 Academy Awards ceremony)

SHOCK PRESS

CANNABIS SMUGGLING BY TROOPS. INVESTIGATION BY JOINT CHIEFS.

Morning Star

STRIP CLUB SHOCK – MAGISTRATES MAY ACT ON INDECENT SHOWS

Daily Mirror

HAVE A BABY? READ 'HOW TO GET FATHER TO HELP'

Cover of *My Baby*

NEW HOME FOR OLD FOLKS IN THE PIPELINE

Barbados *Advocate*

MORE WOMEN NEEDED FOR RANDOM SAMPLING

The Times

QUEEN SEES FONTEYN TAKE 10 CURTAINS

MAN FINED £500 FOR DISCHARGING OIL

The Guardian

A SORDID CASE: HUSBAND NEARLY CUTS HIS WIFE'S HEAD OFF – JUDGE GRANTS SEPARATION

NO WATER, SO FIREMEN IMPROVISED

Liverpool Daily Post

WILSON TAKES OUT HIS CHOPPER

ORGANS OF DEAD BILL PUT TO MPs

Belfast Newsletter

FIREMEN TO SHOW THEIR APPLIANCES TO PASSERS-BY TO ATTRACT RECRUITS

Crawley Advertiser

POLICE FOUND SAFE UNDER BLANKET

Gloucester Echo

REQUEST TO HAVE FAG AT HALF MAST REFUSED

Irish Times

999 MEN CHASE TWO BUSES

Daily Herald – police answering 999 call

8TH ARMY PUSH BOTTLES UP GERMANS

BRISTOL FLOWER GROUP PICK THEIR LEADER

Bristol Evening Post

FEW HAVE ENTERED MISS CARMICHAEL

Headline on lack of support for beauty contest in Carmichael, California

NUDIST NABBED: UNCLOTHED MAN, WHO ADMITS BRANDISHING PISTOL, IS CHARGED WITH CARRYING CONCEALED WEAPON

Providence Journal

MONTY FLIES BACK TO FRONT

BUS ON FIRE – PASSENGERS ALIGHT

West Wales Guardian

Woman's Hour
'What I've Been Doing': Cecilia Bevan,
mother of thirteen children.
(*Radio Times*)

———————○———————

Five red-faced players were forced to take
to the field to demonstrate their ball
control in their Y-fronts.
(The *Wandsworth and Putney Guardian*, reporting
that the Pollygon football team had turned up for a
match minus their shorts)

———————○———————

With the score at six, Knight had Gale lbw,
and eight runs later Preston clipped one of
Eric Russell's balls about 37 yards.
(*Sunday Telegraph*)

———————○———————

Eric Skeels, Stoke's 36-year-old defender,
has been given a free transfer. He played
only four first team games this season after
struggling for long spells with knee and
thing injuries.
(*Birmingham Post*)

———————○———————

An RSPCA inspector commended Mr
Peter Humphrey for saving a goldfish from
drowning.
(*The Times*)

———————○———————

Who shall say howqztNj wodrmf?
(*Manchester Daily Despatch*)

———————○———————

The Night of the Generals
Omar Sharif and Peter O'Toole
The story of a strange manhunt for a
psychopathic kipper set against the
background of wartime Paris.
(*TV Scene*)

———————○———————

Joseph Conrad Walsh, 31, was found guilty of indecent exposure and carrying an offensive weapon when he first appeared at Redbridge Court on March 5.
(*Ilford Recorder*)

Blackburn Times reporter Valerie will not forget the night she danced with Prime Minister Edward Heath at a Young Conservatives' Ball – and ended up in the maternity ward of the local hospital.
(*UK Press Gazette*)

She has a fine, fair skin which, she admits ruefully, comes out in a mass of freckles at the first hint of sin.
(*Essex County Standard*)

The Duchess smashed a bottle of champagne against the bow with unerring aim, and then, while the huge crowd cheered madly, she slid majestically down the greasy slipway into the sea.
(Belfast *News*, reporting the launch of aircraft carrier, *Bulwark*)

Bristol's first league win of the season was a triumph for teenager Kevin Mabbutt who skilfully scored one gal and initiated two more.
(*Sunday Telegraph*)

President Nixon sets off today on a tour of six Asian nations to explain his intentions and assure the countries that America is abandoning them to their enemies.
(*Daily Mirror*)

Nothing gives a greater variety to the appearance of a house than a few undraped widows.
(*House & Garden*)

Sports blackout: France's state-owned television network yesterday cancelled live transmission of two major sporting events, the Spanish Grand Prix and the Rome International Horejumping.
(*Western Mail*)

Philip Hale, music critic on a Boston newspaper, described a concert by the Boston Symphony Orchestra, writing, 'During the performance of this number the kettledrummer sat, like Buddha, regarding his navel.' This appeared in the first edition, but was then spotted by the managing editor who insisted that the word 'navel' should be deleted. The second edition thus read, 'During the performance of this number the kettledrummer sat, like Buddha, regarding his – – – – –.'

A Burnley man was remanded in custody for one week at Burnley Magistrates' Court charged with having sexual intercourse without consent. He was further charged with causing damage to a table.
(*Burnley Express*)

One of Colorado's oldest citizens and a resident of Walsenburg for about a century, died here yesterday. Mrs Quintina was 104 years old at the time of her death, her grandmother said.
(*Enterprise Times*, Brockton, Massachusetts)

Fender was lbw to Townsend, who was bowling round the wicket with four short legs.
(*Daily Telegraph*)

Miss Dorothy Morrison, who was injured by a fall from a horse last week, is in St Joseph's Hospital and covered sufficiently to see her friends.
(*Morristown News*, Morristown, North Dakota)

Gary Watson will read passages selected by Kathleen Raine from 'Beane's Pathetic Books'.
(*BBC Sound Broadcasting News*, 12 November 1957)

Owing to a typing error, 'Blake's Prophetic Books' appeared as 'Beane's Pathetic Books'.
(*BBC Sound Broadcasting News*, 19 November 1957)

Mr George Dobbs of Chertsey is very proud of the fact that he walked 50 miles on a sausage sandwich at the weekend.
(*Staines and Egham News*)

Scorpio (October 23 to November 22): A time when it shows how necessary it is for the true Scorpio male to take himself in hand. If this is done correctly there will be a real burst of activity and pleasure.
(*Lancashire Evening Telegraph*)

Miss Turner has set up a campaign against incestuous relationships at the house in Hydefield Close where she loves with her parents.
(*Enfield Gazette*)

Mr Brown spoke of a possible giant from the Department
of the Environment for repairing the clock.
(*Western Gazette*, Yeovil)

What is more beautiful for the blonde to wear for formal dances than white tulle? My answer – and I'm sure you will agree with me – is 'Nothing'.
(*Evening Gazette*, Worcester, Massachusetts)

———————◇———————

In 1908, she joined the Gaiety Theatre, and married director Lewis Casson – a union that lasted 60 years, producing four children and countless performances.
(*Newsweek*)

———————◇———————

It's a good idea, before you give your hair its nightly brushing, to begin the operation with a brick massage.
(*Ann Arbor News*)

———————◇———————

Why is it, I wonder, that butchers always seem so cheerful? It's not that their job is a specially enviable one, for in winter meat must be very cold to handle. Maybe they get rid of any bad tempers by bashing away with their choppers.
(*Woman's Own*)

———————◇———————

The Civil Service says it is making strenuous efforts to improve the quantity and quality of women.
(*The Guardian*)

———————◇———————

With the unexpected death on February 6 of Qazim Edhem Kastrati, the Albanian community in exile has lost a prominent member.
(*The Times*)

———————◇———————

This amazing cantilever structure [the Forth Bridge] was begun early in 1883 and was opened by Edward, Prince of Wales, on March 4, 1890. The chief engineer was Sir John Fowler and he was assisted by Sir Benjamin Baker on whose shoulders most of the work fell.
(*The People's Friend*)

———————◇———————

Before its late summer departure, the sparrow will build several nests and will bear many little sparrows, judging from past performances.
Mrs Hetherington said that she had not had the same luck with male birds.
(*The Sun*)

———————◇———————

Gen. Graham, who likes to eat as well as any man, would like to see a bit more cor bread ad mustard brees served to the President at the 'wite White House' at this aval submari statio.
'Don't get me wrong,' he cautioned.
(*World Telegraph and Sun*)

———————◇———————

COMMERCIAL BREAKS

Exciting Opportunities for Sales with Knobs and Knockers
(Door furniture firm 'Knobs & Knockers' ad, prior to their opening in Debenhams of Harrow)

Situation Wanted: By young woman 21 years of age. Unusual experience includes three years Necking and Stripping.
(*Shears*, the journal of the American box-making industry)

Wanted: Edible Oil Technologist
(*Observer*)

Infirmary Operatic Society
Male Members Urgently Required
(*Leicester Mercury*)

Head Thrower urgently required. A permanent and well-paid position for the right applicant. Coalport China Ltd.
(*Stoke-on-Trent Evening Sentinel*)

Senior citizen required for light cleaning duties and hovering, 20 hrs weekly.
(*Harrow Observer*)

Wanted: College-type girl to learn kennel
work; feeding, handling, grooming,
stripping; small private kennel; live in.
(*New York Times*)

For Sale: The Devonian Ewe Truss, used by satisfied shepherds for 50 years.
(*Farmers Weekly*)

Towngate Theatre
Until Thursday, 7.30 pm
Woody Allen: Double film feature
Everything You Always Wanted to Know About Sex (X) and *Bananas* (X)
(*Southend Evening Echo*)

Chesham Light Opera Company Presents:
Piddler on the Roof

China Palace Welcomes the Discerning Gourmet
Little Juicy Steamed Bums
a favourite of the Emperor Chien-Lung's
per tray of 10 Buns: Only $3.00
(*The Straits Times*)

Family Planning: Please Use Rear Entrance.
(Sign at Barnstaple Health Centre)

Toilets out of order. Please use Platforms 3-5, 16-20.
(York Station)

What's the difference between a male policeman and a female policeman?
Six inches.
(Police recruiting advert)

This appliance will reduce your hips, or bust.
(*People's Home Journal*)

1928 Rolls-Royce Hearse. Original body.
(*The Times*)

For Sale: 100 year old brass bed. Perfect for antique lover.
(London *Evening Star*)

Mrs and Mrs Charles L. Thompson and Mr and Mrs Russell Hartwick of Tampa will entertain at open house on Sunday, from three until tight.
(Clearwater, Florida, *Sun*)

Apt. to Rent: 86th West – Lady, pleasant, sunny (3 exposures).
(*New York Times*)

Miss Goldhurst has no male goat this season, and refers all clients to Mr Harris.
(*Grantham Journal*)

Signal sent by destroyer to trawler:
WHAT IS THE SIGNIFICANCE OF
THAT SIGNAL YOU ARE FLYING?
Trawler to destroyer:
REGRET I DO NOT KNOW. FLAGS
SMELT OF FISH.
(Reported by Capt. Jack Broome in *Make a Signal*, 1955)

It would be hard to think of a less
appropriate name than the one an
Australian airline chose, Emu Airways.
About the only thing they got right was
that the Emu is an Australian bird;
unfortunately, however, it is completely
incapable of flight.

Grampian Television was originally going
to be called Scottish Highlands & Islands
Television – until someone pointed out that
their initials would not be entirely
appropriate.

The Mutual Screw Company, New York

Daintyfyt Brassiere (Holdings) Ltd.

In the USA, the top of the range of Wang computers is marketed as the 'Wang King'.

After such ethereal names as the Silver Ghost, Cloud, Shadow, Wraith, etc, Rolls-Royce hit on the name 'Mist' for their latest model. Had it been adopted, however, sales to wealthy Germans might have suffered: *mist* in German means 'manure'.

A well-known frozen food company almost called its new product 'Battered Cod Pieces'.

Brains' Frozen Foods' slogan, 'Faggots – Great Balls of Goodness' astonished Americans to whom the term 'faggot' is used only to mean a person of homosexual persuasion. Persons of that leaning avidly collect packets and posters displaying this intriguing message.

There is a Finnish lock-deicer called Piss.

Fearing that the title of the 1944 British film, *Fanny by Gaslight,* might be misconstrued in the USA (where a fanny is a bottom), it was altered to *Man of Evil.* The alternative (and far more vulgar) meaning of 'fanny' did not even occur to the British distributors.

The 1940 US film *The Bank Dick,* starring W. C. Fields, became *The Bank Detective* in GB, while the 1950 *Young Man with a Horn* became *Young Man of Music.*

In Australia, Sellotape is called Durex. Australians wishing to buy sticky tape in England have the same sort of problems as English people attempting to buy condoms in Australia.

Cona coffee percolators realised in the nick of time that they could not use their name in Portuguese-speaking countries, where *cona* is a vulgar word for 'vagina'. So in these countries they call their product *Acolon* instead.

In Portugal the defunct Foden truck company's products were called Poden – Foden means 'f***'.

DR SPOONER AND MR GOLDWYN

SPOONERISMS

Perpetrated by – or attributed to – Oxford dean, Rev. W. A. Spooner (1844-1930)
(Who disclaimed them – putting them down to "the woolish fit of the undergraduates")

The defeated parliamentary candidate has just received
a blushing crow.

You are always hissing at my mystery lessons.

A well-boiled icicle.

We all know what it is to have a half-warmed fish within us.
(a half-formed wish)

Yes, indeed; the Lord is a shoving leopard.

Son, it is kisstomery to cuss the bride.

One swell foop.

You have tasted two worms. You will leave Oxford by the town drain.

Marden me, padam, aren't you occupewing the wrong pie?
May I sew you to another sheet?

When I tried to stroke it (a kitten), it popped on its drawers
and ran out of the room.

(Asked what he would like for dessert) I think I should like
a little of that stink puff.

(Introducing Mrs Ironside-Bax) Professor, I should like you
to meet a friend of mine, Mrs Iron Backside.

GOLDWYNISMS

*Created by American film producer Sam Goldwyn (1882-1974)
– whose original name was Samuel Goldfish.*

Why did you name your baby Arthur? Every Tom, Dick and
Harry is called Arthur.

We can get all the Indians we need at the reservoir.

In two words: impossible.

It's more than magnificent – it's mediocre.

It's spreading like wildflowers.

Let's have some new clichés.

A bachelor's life is no life for a single man.

Anybody who goes to see a psychiatrist ought to have his
head examined.

If Roosevelt were alive, he'd turn in his grave.

(Told that a story was caustic) I don't care what it costs –
if it's good, we'll make it.

Include me out.

(To friends seeing *him* off on a liner) Bon voyage!

What we want is a story that starts with an earthquake
and works it way up to a climax.

Every director bites the hand that lays the golden eggs.

The trouble with this business is the dearth of bad pictures.

If I could drop dead right now, I'd be the happiest man alive!

(During filming of *The Last Supper*) Why only twelve
disciples? Go out and get thousands.

You ought to take the bull by the teeth.

I'd be sticking my head into a moose.

This makes me so sore it gets my dandruff up.

If you can't give me your word of honour, will you give me
your promise?

A verbal contract isn't worth the paper it's written on.

Who wants to go out and see a bad movie when they can stay at home and see a bad one free on TV?

Tell me, how did you love the picture?

Let's bring it up to date with some snappy nineteenth-century dialogue.

(On being told that he might have problems in filming a certain play, since the leading female character was a lesbian) That's all right – we can change her into an Italian.

We have all passed a lot of water since then.

(To Laurence Olivier on the day the atom bomb was dropped on Hiroshima) You know, Larry, that atom bomb is dynamite!

I'll give you a definite maybe.

What beautiful hands your wife has!
Yes, I'm going to have a bust made of them.

LAST WORDS

I suffered so much from printers' errors,
That death for me can hold no terrors.
No doubt this stone has been misdated –
Oh, how I wish I'd been cremated.
(Daniel George, *Epitaph for a Dead Author*)

Erected to the Memory of
John McFarlane
Drown'd in the Water of Leith
By a few affectionate friends.
(Edinburgh)

————◇————

To the Memory
of
Abraham Beaulieu
Born 15 September
1822
Accidentally shot
4th April 1844
As a mark of affection
from his brother.
(La Pointe, Wisconsin)

Richard Kendrick
Was buried August 29th, 1785,
By the desire of his wife,
Margaret Kendrick.
(Wroxham, Norfolk)

Here lies the body of James Vernon, Esq.,
only surviving son of Admiral Vernon;
died 23rd July, 1723.
(St Andrew's, Plymouth)

Here lies W.S. Died 14th May 1843.
All his life he loved sailors.
(Sonning, Berkshire)

The Body of Henry Rogers
A painfull preacher in this church
Two and thirty years.
(Selmeston, Sussex)

On 8th August 1912, he left us in peace.
(San Michele, Venice)

Stop here, ye Gay
& ponder what ye doeth
Blue lightnings flew &
Swiftly seized my Breath
A more tremendous
flash will fill the skies
When I and all that sleep in death shall rise
(Simon Willard, d. 1766, Sheffield, Massachusetts)

Here lies John Higley,
Whose father and mother were drowned
On their passage from America.
Had they both lived, they would have been
Buried here too.
(Belturbet, Co. Cavan, Ireland)

Sacred to the memory of
Major James Brush, Royal Artillery,
who was killed by the accidental discharge
of a pistol by his orderly, 14th April, 1831.
Well done, good and faithful servant.
(Woolwich, London)

THE END